Core Knowledge Language Arts®

Unit 7
Workbook

Skills Strand
KINDERGARTEN

Amplify learning.

Core Knowledge®

Unit 7
Workbook

This Workbook contains worksheets that accompany many of the lessons from the Teacher Guide for Unit 7. Each worksheet is identified by the lesson number in which it is used. The worksheets in this book do not include written instructions for students because the instructions would have words that are not decodable. Teachers will explain these worksheets to the students orally, using the instructions in the Teacher Guide. The Workbook is a student component, which means each student should have a Workbook.

Name _____

Directions: Have students trace and copy the digraph and word and say the sounds while printing.

lun**ch**   bran**ch**

ben**ch**   **ch**ips

Directions: Have students write each word under its matching picture.

Directions: For each picture, have students circle the spelling of the depicted item and write the name of the item on the line.

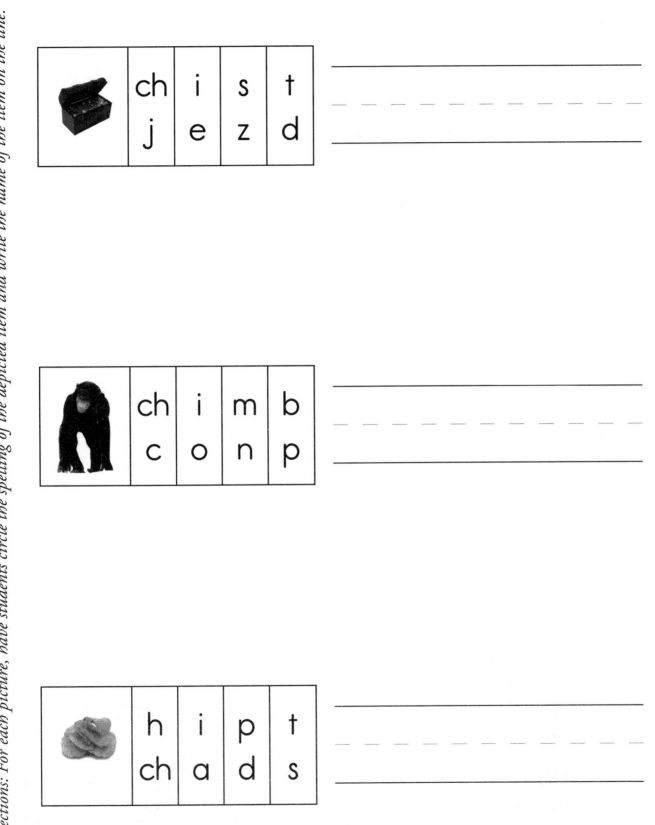

ch	i	s	t
j	e	z	d

ch	i	m	b
c	o	n	p

h	i	p	t
ch	a	d	s

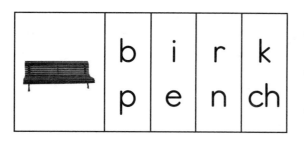

	b	i	r	k
	p	e	n	ch

_____
- - - - - - - - - - - - - -
_____

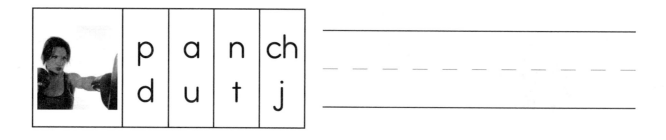

	p	a	n	ch
	d	u	t	j

_____
- - - - - - - - - - - - - -
_____

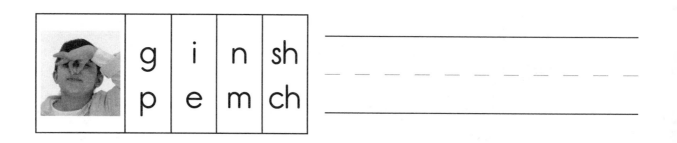

	g	i	n	sh
	p	e	m	ch

_____
- - - - - - - - - - - - - -
_____

Directions: Have students trace and copy the digraph and word and say the sounds while printing.

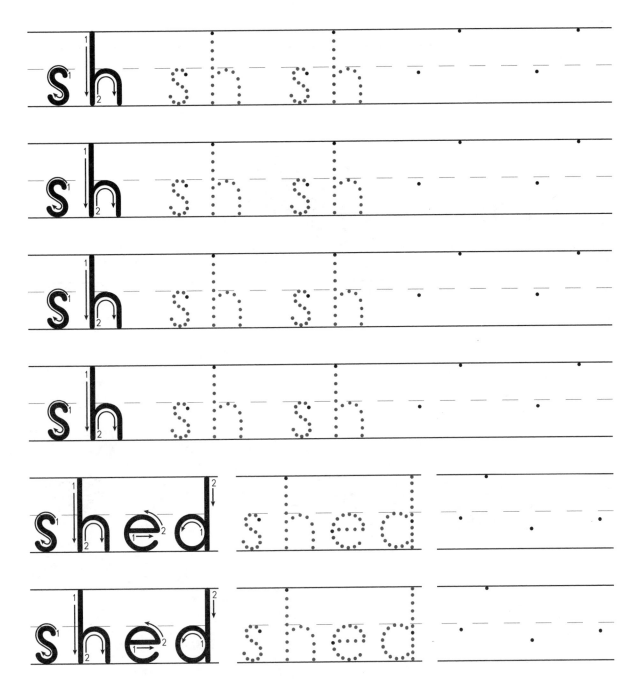

1. **sh**in

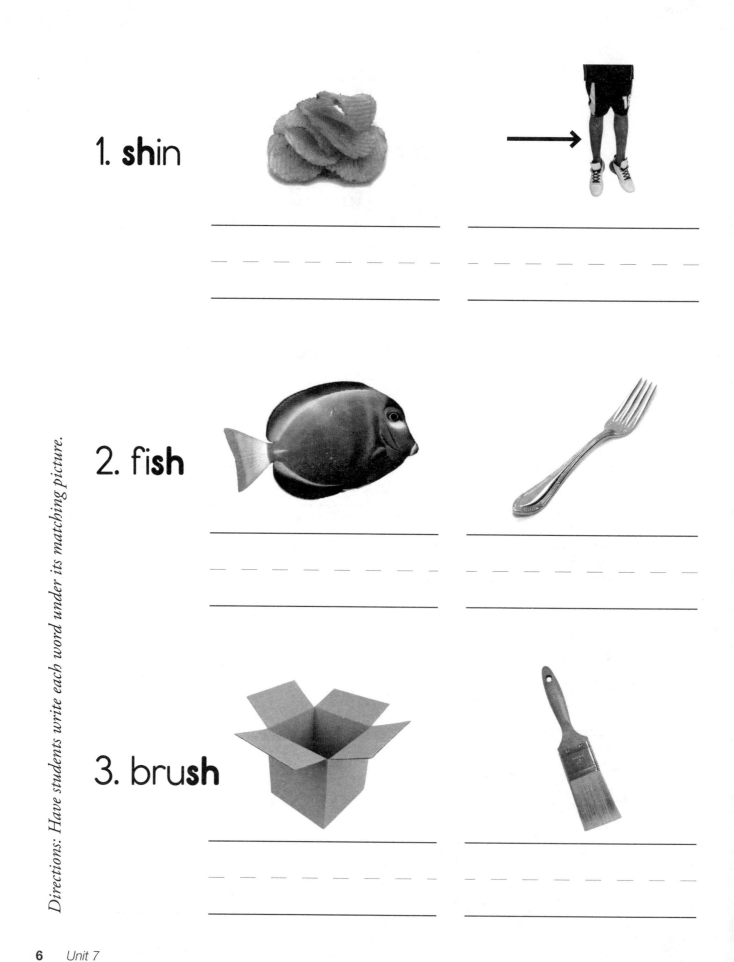

2. fi**sh**

3. bru**sh**

Dear Family Member,

Your child has been taught to read the digraphs 'sh' and 'ch'. Digraphs are spellings consisting of two letters. Both letters together stand for only one sound as in "<u>ch</u>ill" and "ra<u>sh</u>." Words with digraphs are difficult to read at first because the reader has to recognize that two letters combined stand for a single sound. Ask your child to cut out the word cards. Show the cards to your child and have your child read them. Notice the digraphs are printed in bold letters; if necessary, remind your child these two letters stand for just one sound. You may also read the words aloud and have your child write the sounds down, one at a time. Please keep these cards for future practice.

ben**ch**	**ch**est	fi**sh**
chin	**sh**rubs	**sh**ed
chips	spla**sh**	crun**ch**
tra**sh**	cru**sh**	**ch**imps

Directions: For each picture, have students read the phrases and put a check mark in the box next to the matching phrase.

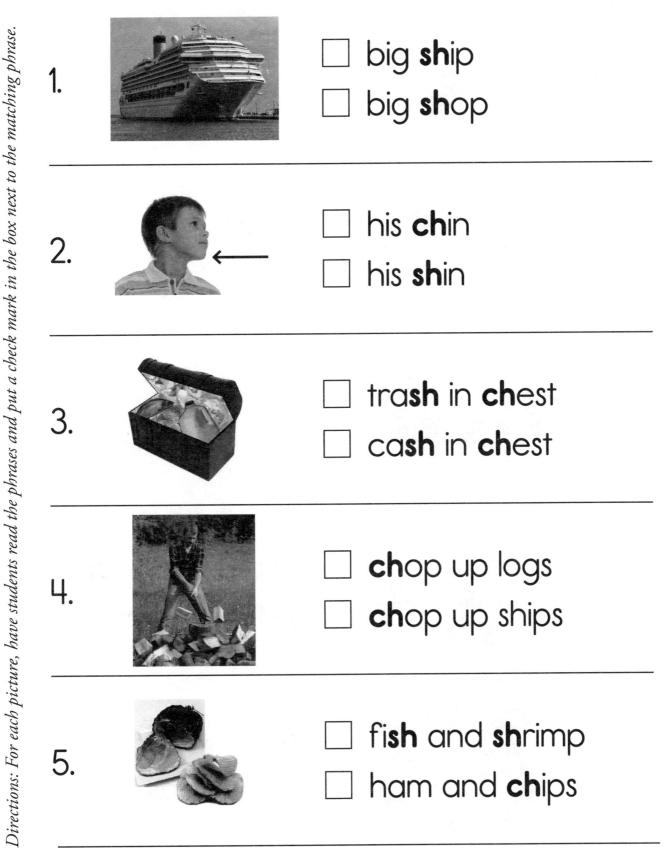

1. ☐ big **sh**ip
   ☐ big **sh**op

2. ☐ his **ch**in
   ☐ his **sh**in

3. ☐ tra**sh** in **ch**est
   ☐ ca**sh** in **ch**est

4. ☐ **ch**op up logs
   ☐ **ch**op up ships

5. ☐ fi**sh** and **sh**rimp
   ☐ ham and **ch**ips

6. ☐ su**ch** big hands
   ☐ su**ch** big lips

7. ☐ cru**sh** can
   ☐ cru**sh** box

8. ☐ dog on ben**ch**
   ☐ cat on ben**ch**

9. ☐ crab can pin**ch**
   ☐ kid can pin**ch**

10. ☐ mom **sh**ops
    ☐ dad **sh**ops

Name _____

Dear Family Member,

   For each row on the front and back, have your child blend and read all three words and circle the word matching the picture. If necessary, identify the pictures for your child.

1.   **ch**amp   **ch**omp   **ch**imp

2.   pun**ch**   hun**ch**   bun**ch**

3.   **sh**ed   mu**sh**   sa**sh**

4.   **ch**ip   **sh**ip   **sh**in

5. bran**ch**   ran**ch**   brand

6. lun**ch**   hun**ch**   lump

7. **sh**elf   fi**sh**   **sh**rug

8. cra**sh**   trap   tra**sh**

9. **sh**ip   **sh**in   **ch**in

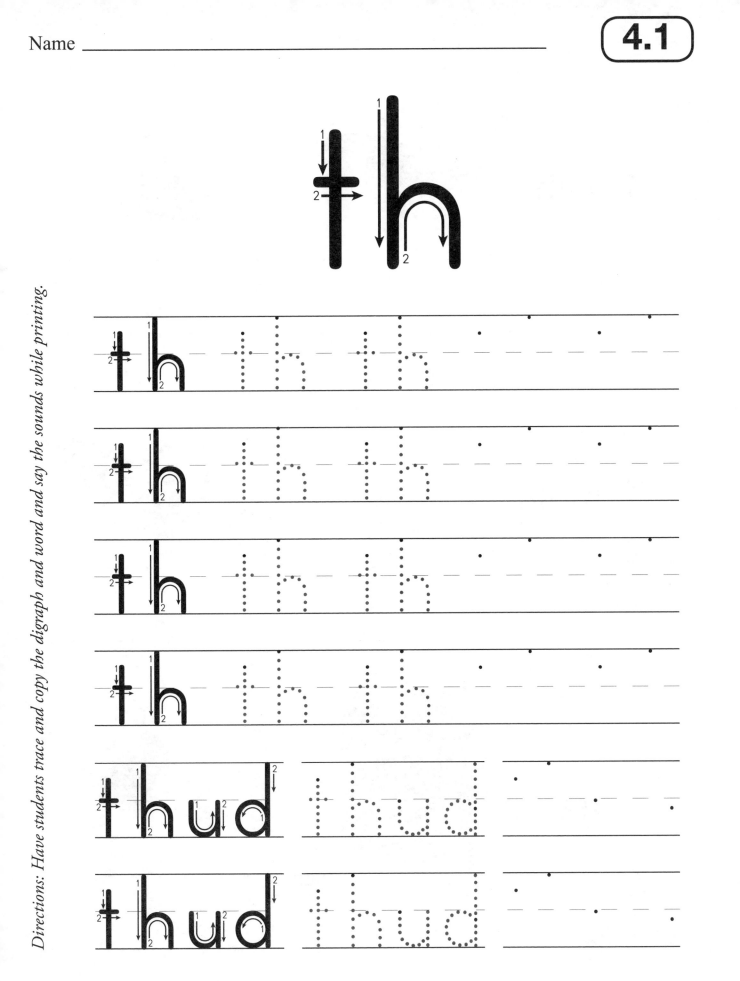

Directions: Have students trace and copy the digraph and word and say the sounds while printing.

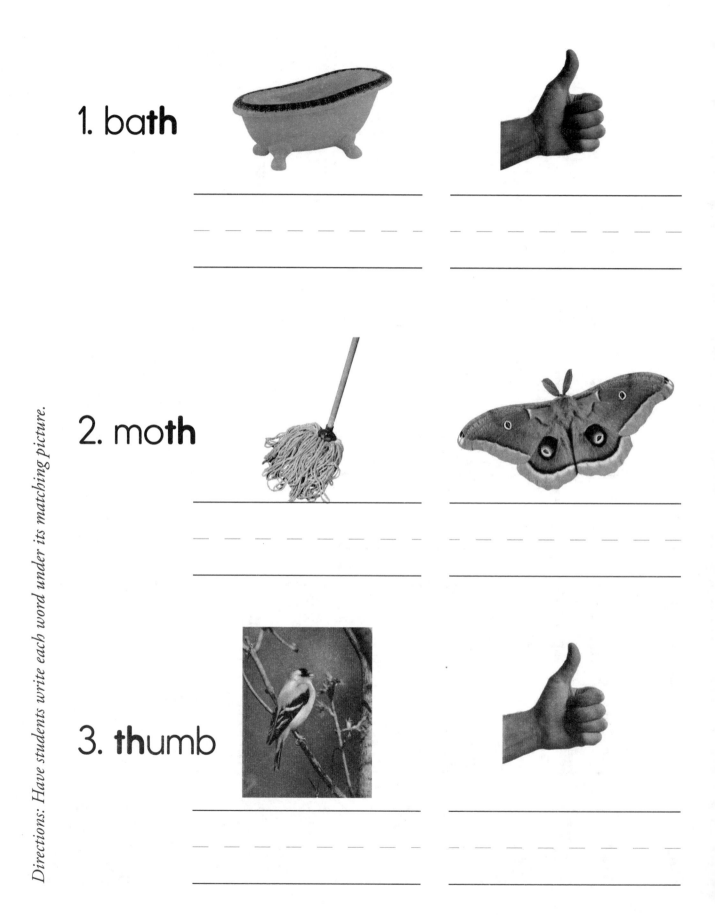

1. ba**th**

2. mo**th**

3. **th**umb

Directions: Have students trace and copy the digraph and word and say the sounds while printing.

| math | than | then | theft |
| that | this | bath | thin |

Directions: Have students write the words with buzzy /th/ under the bee saying "bzzzz" and the words with non-buzzy /th/ under the crossed-out bee.

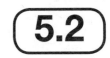

Dear Family Member,

On the front and back of this sheet, have your child draw a line from each word on the left to the matching picture. If necessary, identify the pictures for your child.

1. ba**th**

2. fi**sh**

3. **th**umb

4. bran**ch**

5. mo**th**

6. bru**sh**

7. **ch**op

8. pin**ch**

9. **ch**est

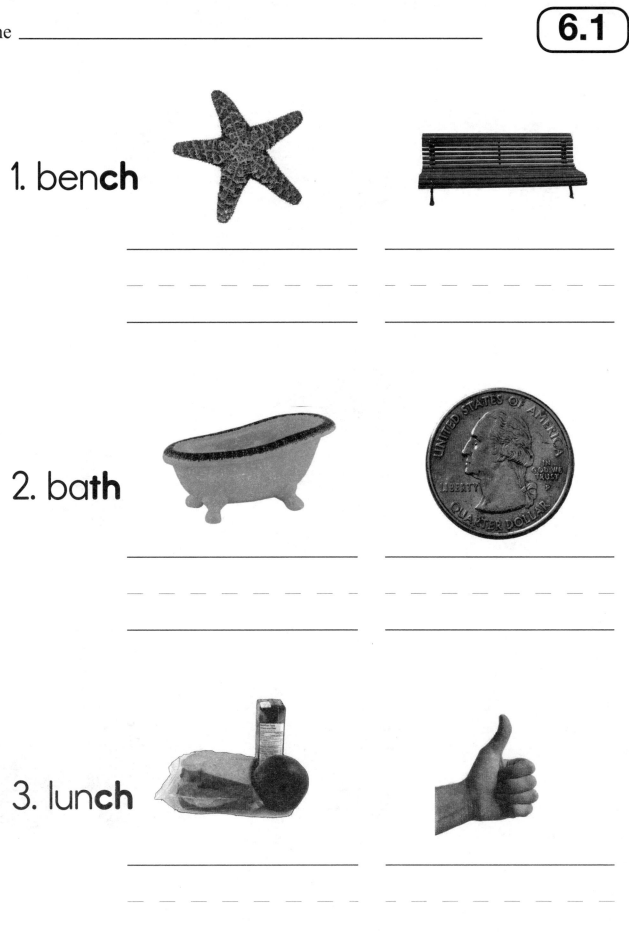

Directions: Have students write each word under its matching picture.

1. ben**ch**

2. ba**th**

3. lun**ch**

4. mo**th**

5. ca**sh**

6. pun**ch**

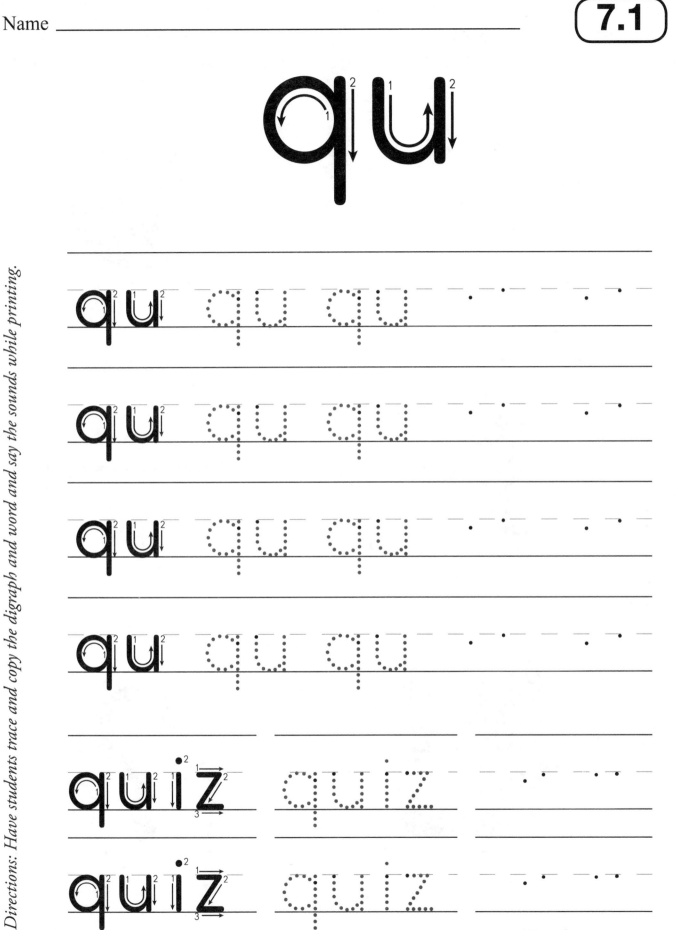

Directions: Have students trace and copy the digraph and word and say the sounds while printing.

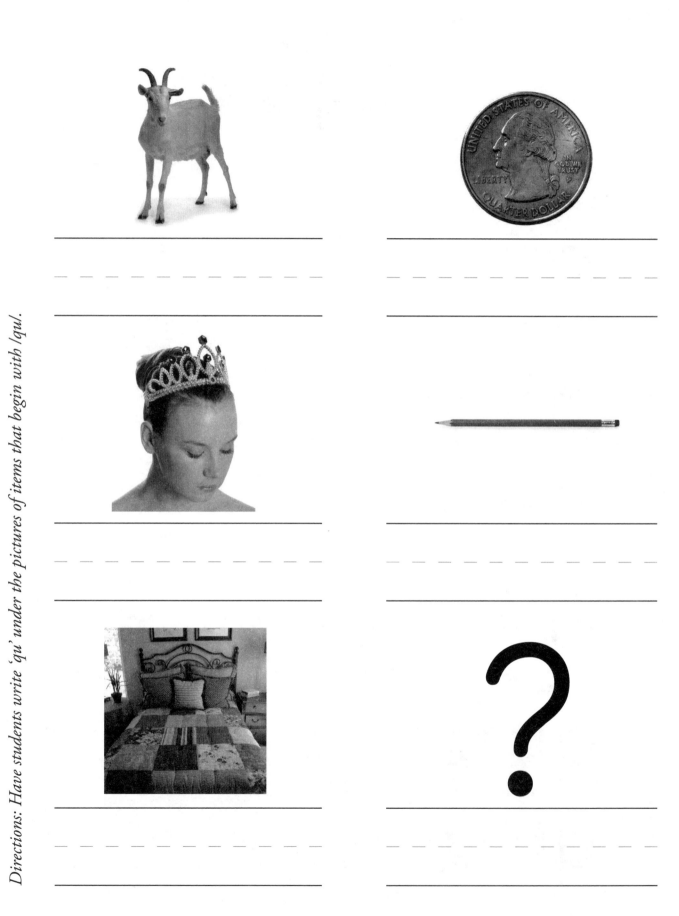

Directions: Have students write 'qu' under the pictures of items that begin with /qu/.

Dear Family Member,

Ask your child to cut out the two circles. Pin the smaller circle on top of the larger circle with a brass fastener. Ask your child to spin the smaller circle to make words. Have your child read the words he or she makes. You may ask your child to copy the words on a sheet of paper.

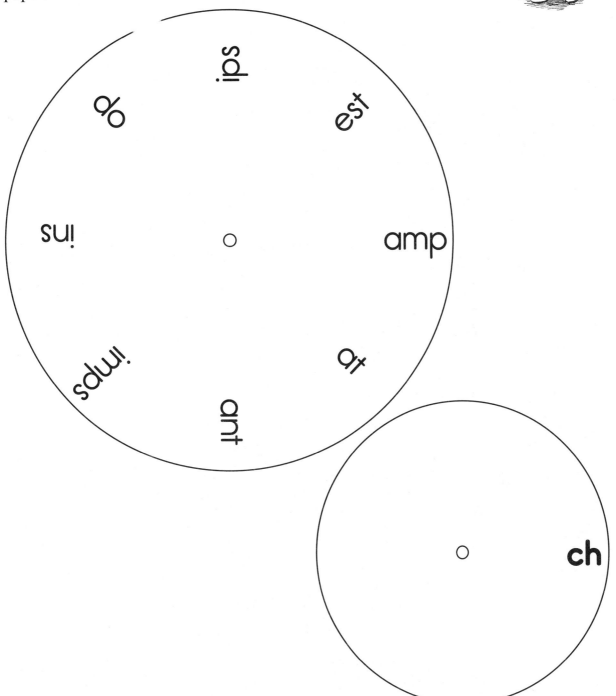

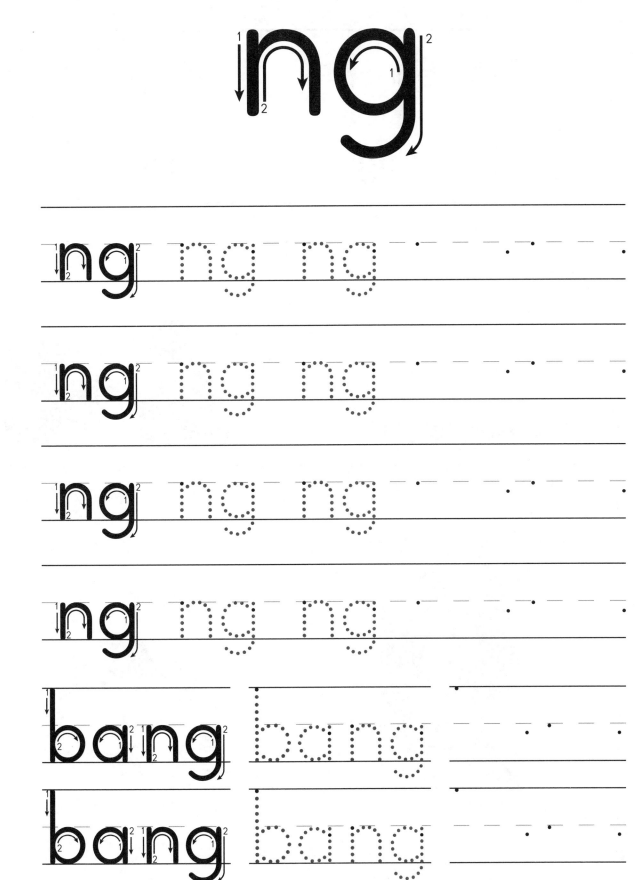

Directions: Have students trace and copy the digraph and word and say the sounds while printing.

punch   king

ring   swing

© 2013 Core Knowledge Foundation

Directions: Have students write each word under its matching picture.

Directions: Have students hold up this worksheet when you say /n/.

n

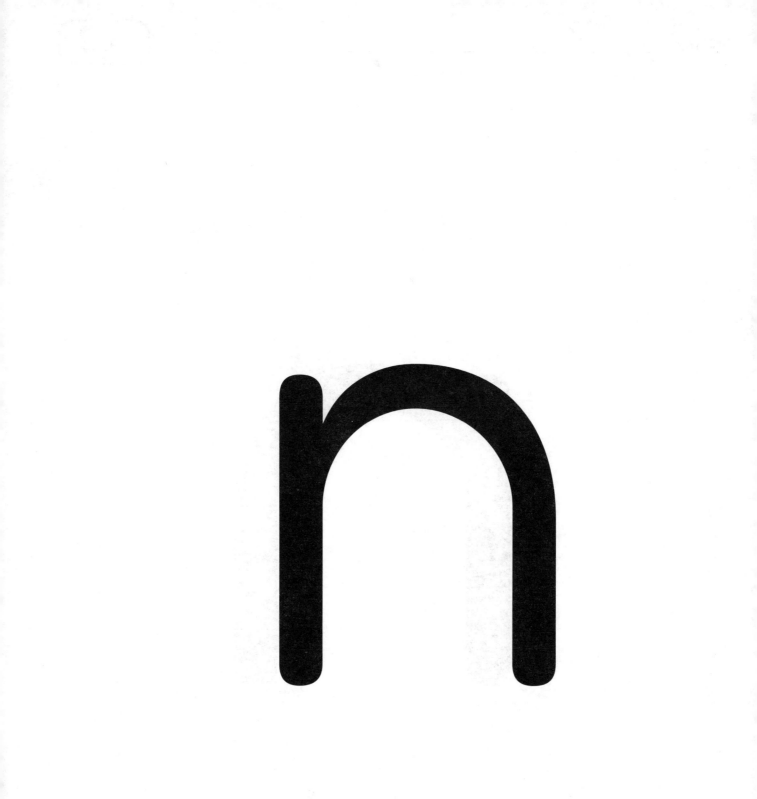

Directions: Have students hold up this worksheet when you say /ng/.

ng

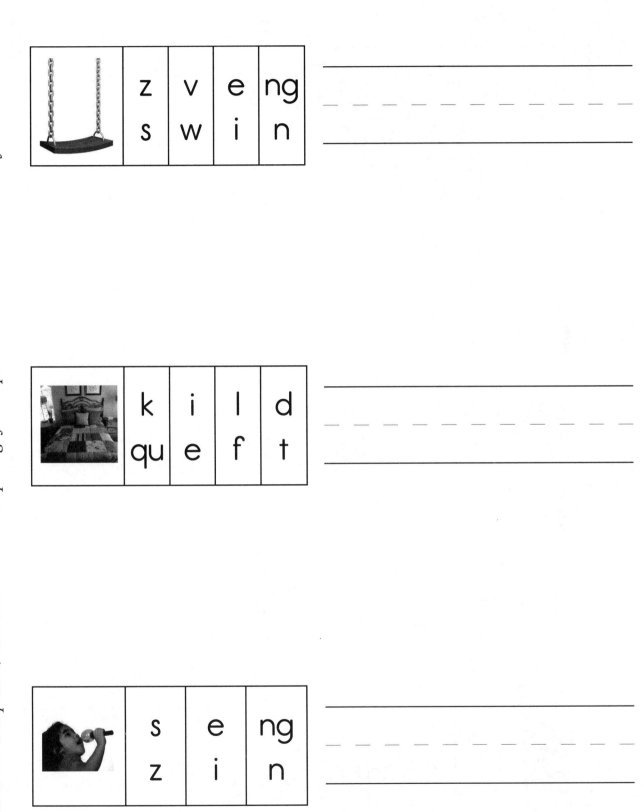

Directions: For each picture, have students circle the spelling of the depicted item and write the name of the item on the line.

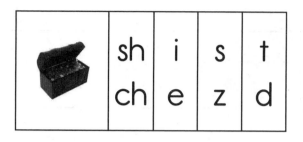

sh	i	s	t
ch	e	z	d

_____

- - - - - - - - - - - - -

_____

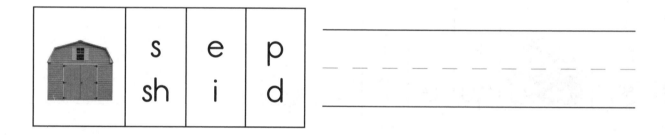

s	e	p
sh	i	d

_____

- - - - - - - - - - - - -

_____

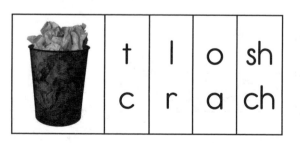

t	l	o	sh
c	r	a	ch

_____

- - - - - - - - - - - - -

_____

Name ______________________________ 9.1

Directions: For each word, have students circle and count the sounds. Have students write the number of sounds in the box and copy the word on the line.

1. ran**ch** ☐ ____________

2. **sh**ip ☐ ____________

3. plu**sh** ☐ ____________

4. ba**th** ☐ ____________

5. **ch**ips ☐ ____________

6. **th**is ☐ ____________

7. so**ng** ☐ ____________

8. **th**em

9. mo**th**

10. si**ng**

11. ben**ch**

12. bru**sh**

13. **ch**est

14. **th**ing

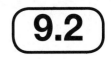

Dear Family Member,

Your child is learning to read the digraphs 'sh', 'ch', 'qu', 'th', and 'ng'. Digraphs are spellings consisting of two letters. Both letters together stand for only one sound. Ask your child to cut out the word cards. Show the cards to your child and have your child read them. You may ask your child to copy the words onto a sheet of paper. You may also read the words aloud and have your child write the sounds down, one at a time. Please keep these cards and practice reading them each night.

wi**sh**	su**ch**	**th**is
quilt	**sh**ip	ba**th**
stri**ng**	**th**at	**qu**iz
mu**ch**	in**ch**	**th**ing
them	**th**en	wi**th**

1. **th**en   **th**in

2. so**ng**   sa**ng**

3. gu**sh**   lu**sh**

4. **ch**at   **ch**ant

5. **th**ing   **th**in

6. **qu**it   **qu**ilt

Directions: Have students circle the dictated words and copy them on the lines.

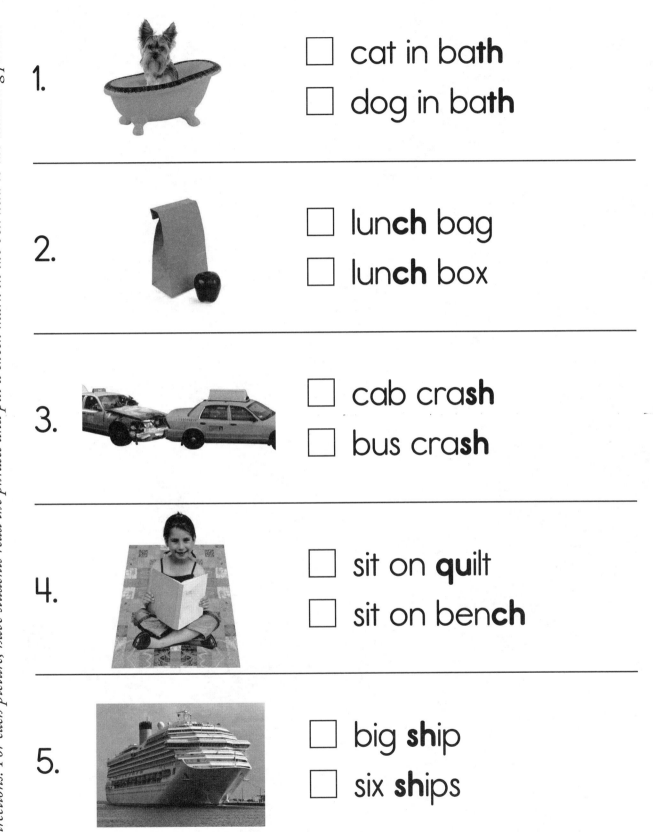

1. ☐ cat in ba**th**
   ☐ dog in ba**th**

2. ☐ lun**ch** bag
   ☐ lun**ch** box

3. ☐ cab cra**sh**
   ☐ bus cra**sh**

4. ☐ sit on **qu**ilt
   ☐ sit on ben**ch**

5. ☐ big **sh**ip
   ☐ six **sh**ips

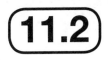

Student Record Sheet – Reading Words with Consonant Digraphs

Note: The number in parentheses represents the number of points/sounds in each word.

	Word						Total Phonemes Correct
1.	then	/th/	/e/	/n/			_____ (3)
2.	path	/p/	/a/	/th/			_____ (3)
3.	chin	/ch/	/i/	/n/			_____ (3)
4.	lunch	/l/	/u/	/n/	/ch/		_____ (4)
5.	thrash	/th/	/r/	/a/	/sh/		_____ (4)
6.	quilts	/qu/	/i/	/l/	/t/	/s/	_____ (5)
7.	ring	/r/	/i/	/ng/			_____ (3)
8.	shut	/sh/	/u/	/t/			_____ (3)
9.	song	/s/	/o/	/ng/			_____ (3)
10.	quiz	/qu/	/i/	/z/			_____ (3)

Initial Digraphs _____ /6   Final Digraphs _____ /5   **Total Correct** _____ /34

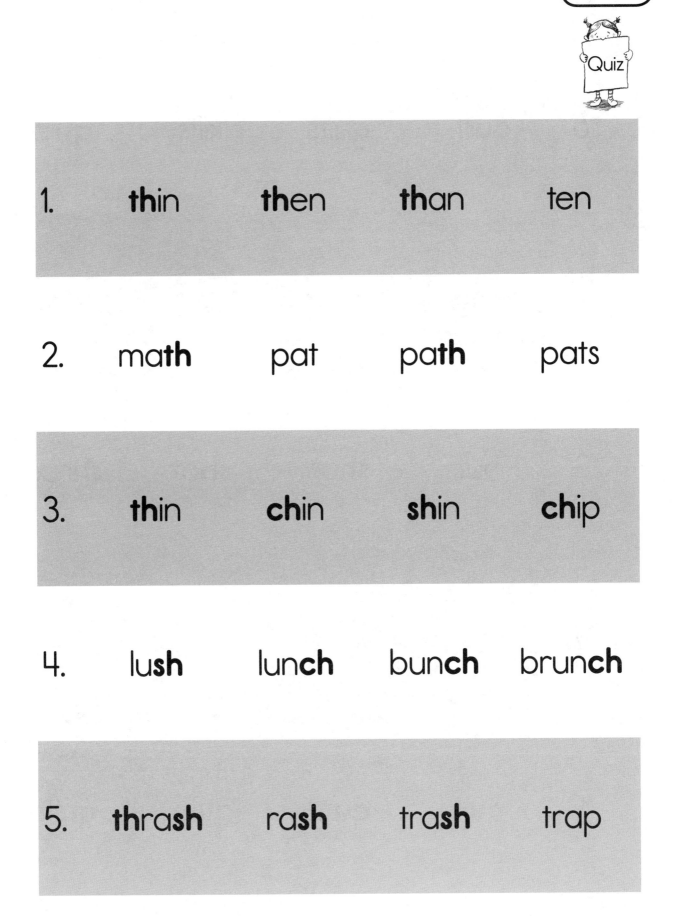

1. **th**in   **th**en   **th**an   ten

2. ma**th**   pat   pa**th**   pats

3. **th**in   **ch**in   **sh**in   **ch**ip

4. lu**sh**   lun**ch**   bun**ch**   brun**ch**

5. **th**ra**sh**   ra**sh**   tra**sh**   trap

6. **qu**ilts   **qu**its   kilts   **qu**ip

7. si**ng**   ra**ng**   ri**ng**   ru**ng**

8. hut   **sh**ut   **sh**ot   **sh**rug

9. go**ng**   soft   so**ng**   si**ng**

10. **qu**it   **qu**iz   **qu**ip   **qu**its

Seth

This is Se**th** Smi**th**.
Se**th** is ten.

Se**th** must get in bed at ten.
Se**th** can jump on his bed,
but not past ten.
Se**th** can stomp and romp
and stand on his hands, but
not past ten.

Se**th**'s dad gets mad if
Se**th** is not in bed at ten.

Sing the ABC song with your child, as he or she points to each letter. When you finish, randomly call out a letter by name and ask your child to touch it.

a b c d e f g

h i j k l m n

o p q r s t u

v w x y z

| **sh**ed | stri**ng** | **qu**ilt |
| pun**ch** | ben**ch** | pa**th** |

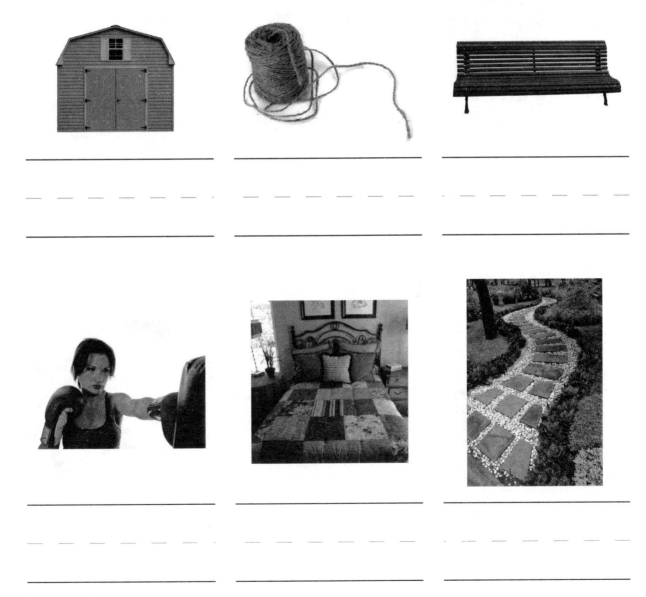

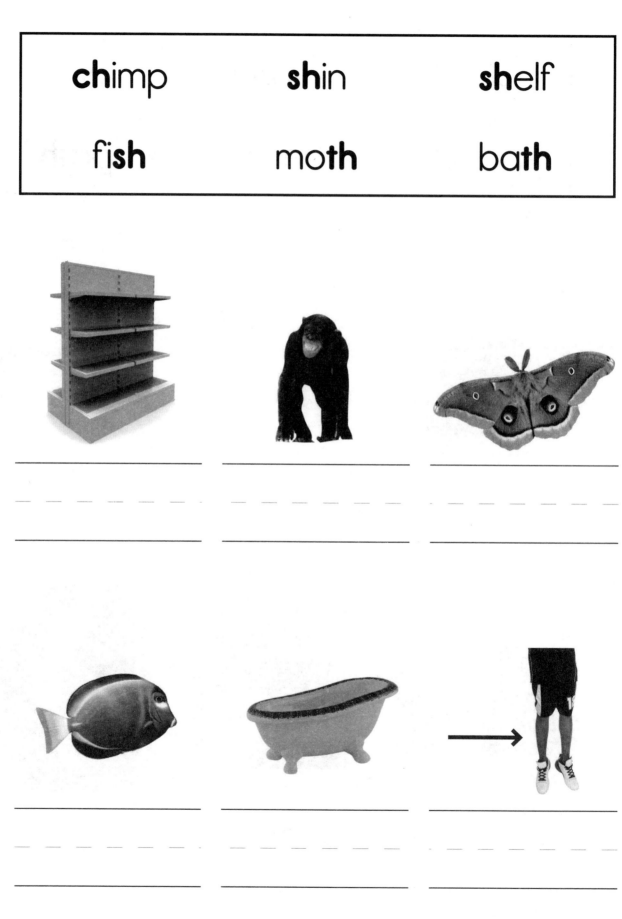

chimp	shin	shelf
fish	moth	bath

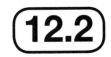

Dear Family Member,

This is a story your child has read at school. Encourage your child to read the story to you, and then talk about it together. Encourage your child to ask *you* questions about the story.

Seth's Mom

This is Pat.
Pat is **Seth**'s mom.

Pat can fix **thing**s.

Pat can scrub, plan, and
think.

Pat can run fast.

Pat can si**ng** so**ng**s.

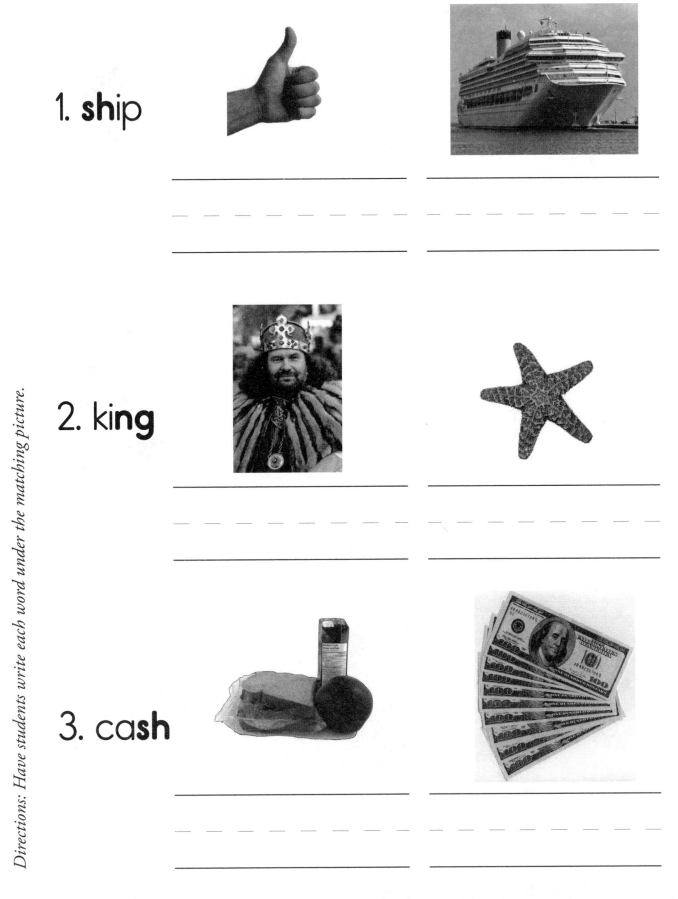

Directions: Have students write each word under the matching picture.

1. **sh**ip

2. ki**ng**

3. ca**sh**

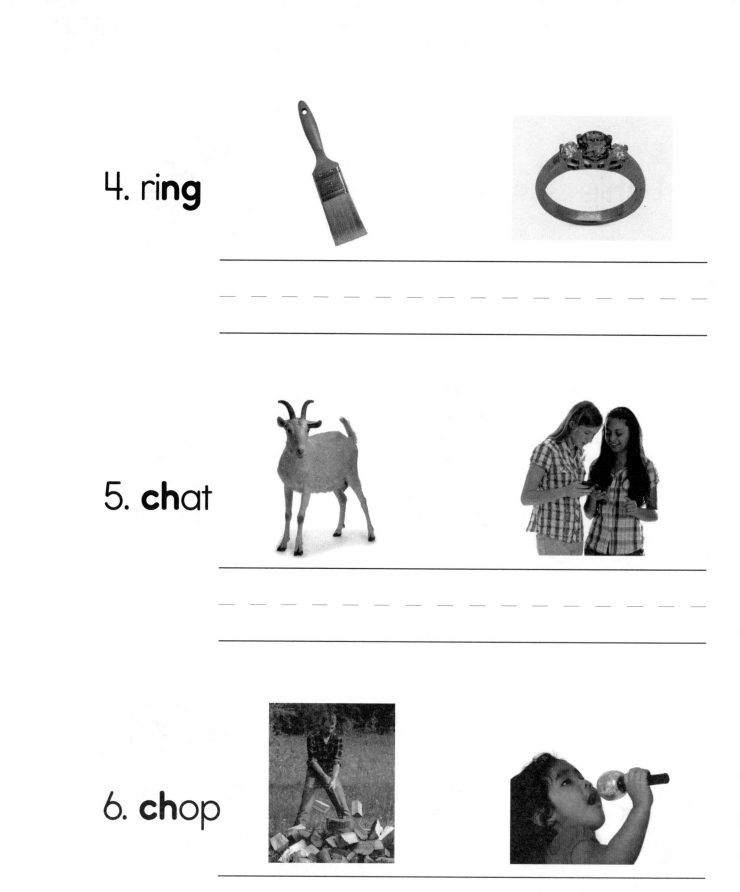

4. ri**ng**

5. **ch**at

6. **ch**op

Dear Family Member,

This is a story your child has read at school. Encourage your child to read the story to you, and then talk about it together.

Seth's Dad

This is Ted.
Ted is **Seth**'s dad.
Ted is stro**ng**.

Ted can **ch**op big logs
wi**th** his ax.

Ted can lift big stumps.

Ted can cru**sh** tin cans
wi**th** his hands.

Name _____

Directions: For each picture, have students circle the spelling of the depicted item and write the name of the item on the line.

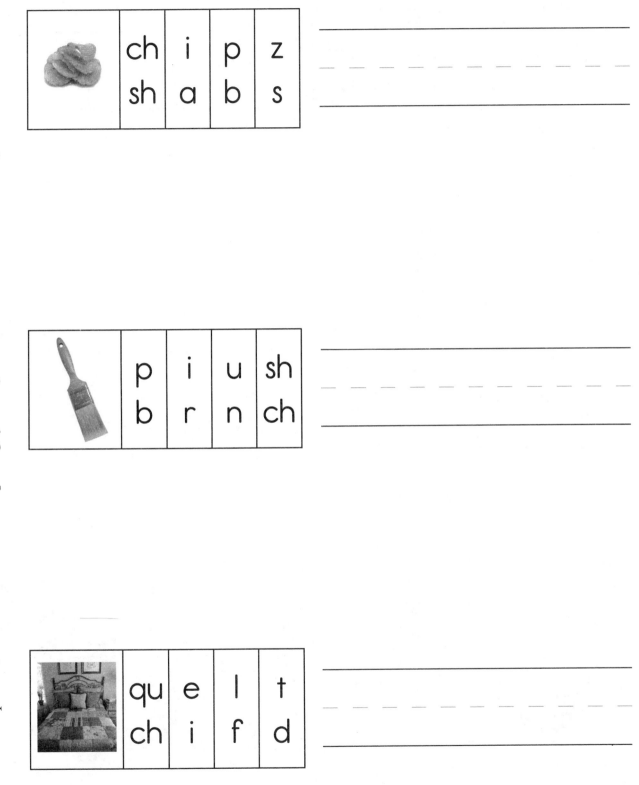

ch	i	p	z
sh	a	b	s

_____

p	i	u	sh
b	r	n	ch

_____

qu	e	l	t
ch	i	f	d

_____

| m | i | ch |
| n | o | th |

_____

- - - - - - - - - - -

_____

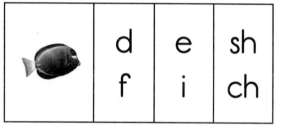

| d | e | sh |
| f | i | ch |

_____

- - - - - - - - - - -

_____

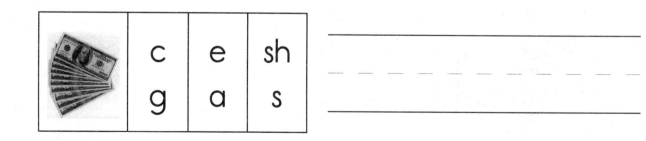

| c | e | sh |
| g | a | s |

_____

- - - - - - - - - - -

_____

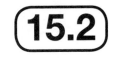

Dear Family Member,

This is a story your child has read at school. Encourage your child to read the story to you, and then talk about it together.

Sal's Fish Shop

Pat and S**e**th went in Sal's
Fi**sh Sh**op.

Sal had fre**sh** fi**sh**.
Sal had fre**sh sh**rimp.
Sal had crabs.
Sal had clams.
Sal had **squ**id.

Pat got fi**sh** and **sh**rimp.

Sing the ABC song with your child, as he or she points to each letter. When you finish, randomly call out letters by name and ask your child to touch the letter you named.

a   b   c   d   e   f   g

h   i   j   k   l   m   n

o   p   q   r   s   t   u

v   w   x   y   z

© 2013 Core Knowledge Foundation

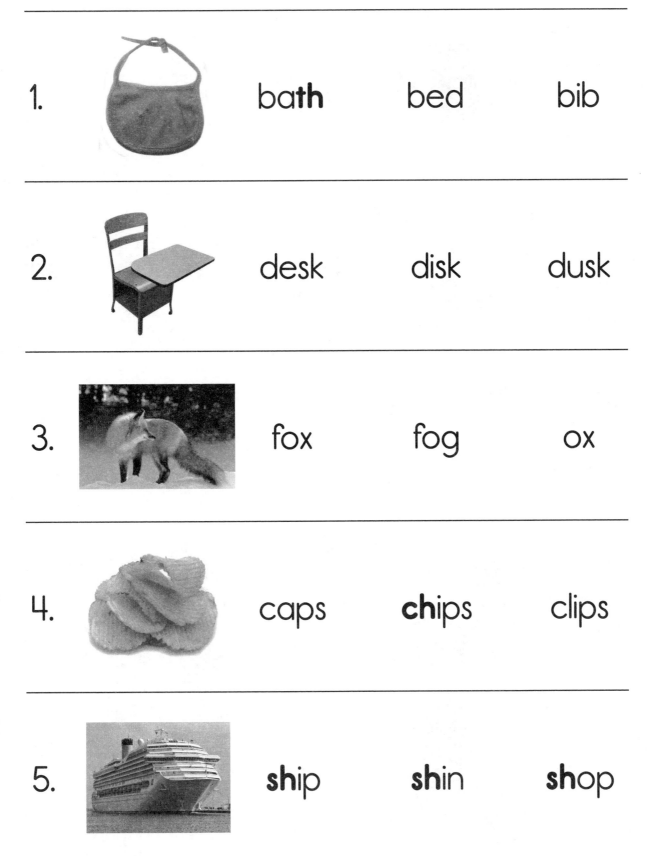

1. **bath**   bed   bib

2. desk   disk   dusk

3. fox   fog   ox

4. caps   **ch**ips   clips

5. **sh**ip   **sh**in   **sh**op

Directions: For each picture, have students circle the matching word.

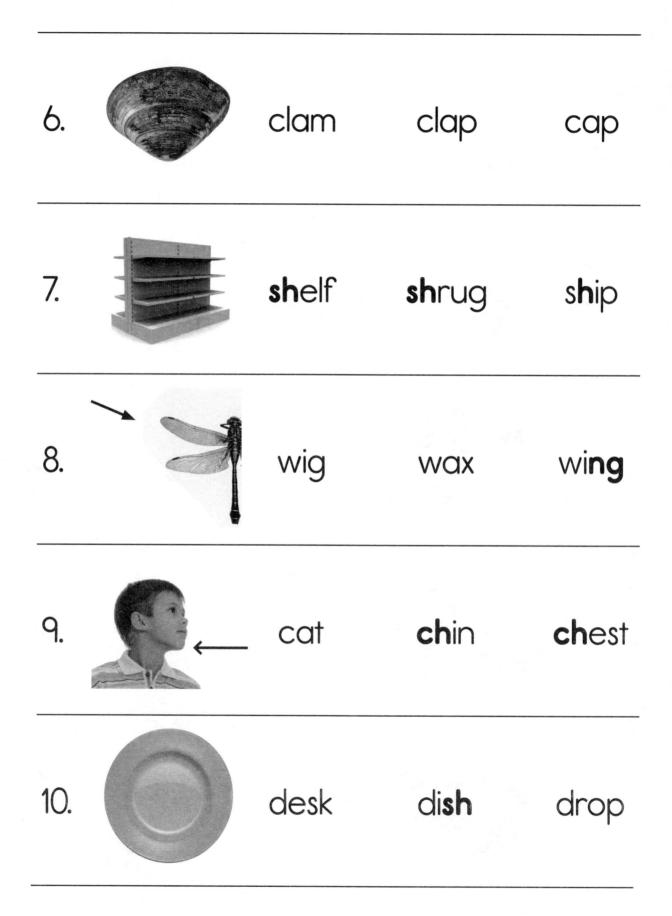

6. clam   clap   cap

7. **sh**elf   **sh**rug   **sh**ip

8. wig   wax   wi**ng**

9. cat   **ch**in   **ch**est

10. desk   di**sh**   drop

Name _____

Dear Family Member,

On the front and back of this sheet have your child write each word under the matching picture. If necessary, identify the pictures for your child.

1. si**ng**

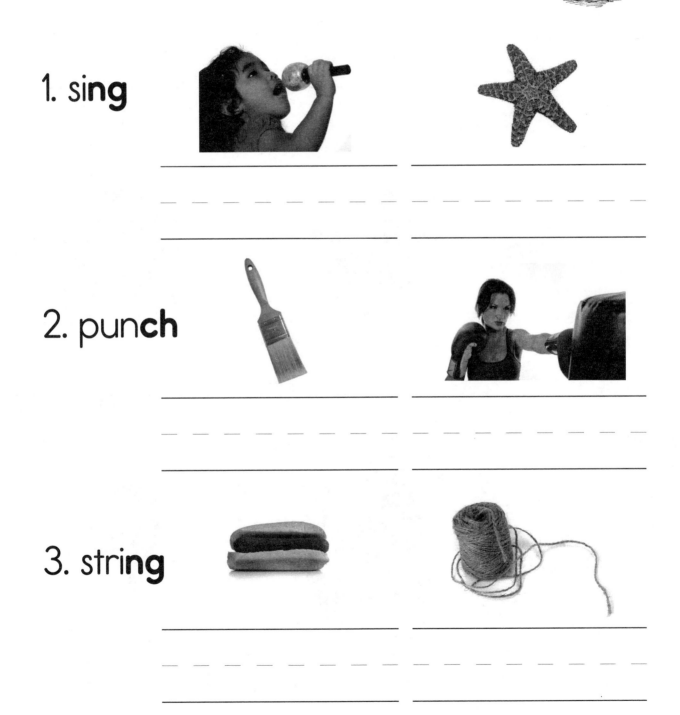

2. pun**ch**

3. stri**ng**

4. ki**ng**

_____   _____

- - - - - - - - - - - - - - - - - - -   - - - - - - - - - - - - - - - - - - -

_____   _____

5. di**sh**

_____   _____

- - - - - - - - - - - - - - - - - - -   - - - - - - - - - - - - - - - - - - -

_____   _____

6. **qu**ilt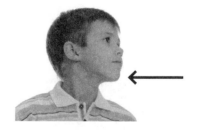

_____   _____

- - - - - - - - - - - - - - - - - - -   - - - - - - - - - - - - - - - - - - -

_____   _____

Directions: For each picture, have students read the phrases and put a check mark in the box next to the matching phrase.

1. ☐ lo**ng** belt
   ☐ lo**ng** stri**ng**

2. ☐ tra**sh** bag
   ☐ tra**sh** can

3. ☐ man on ben**ch**
   ☐ kid on ben**ch**

4. ☐ pig wi**th** hen
   ☐ pig wi**th** bug

5. ☐ bru**sh** on **sh**elf
   ☐ bru**sh** on bed

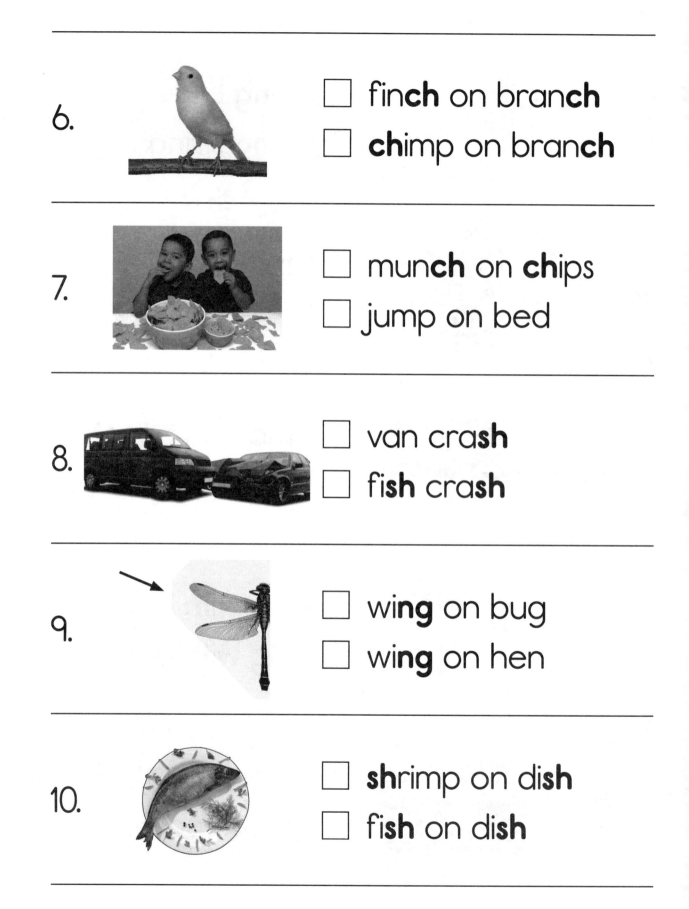

6. ☐ fin**ch** on bran**ch**
   ☐ **ch**imp on bran**ch**

7. ☐ mun**ch** on **ch**ips
   ☐ jump on bed

8. ☐ van cra**sh**
   ☐ fi**sh** cra**sh**

9. ☐ wi**ng** on bug
   ☐ wi**ng** on hen

10. ☐ **sh**rimp on di**sh**
    ☐ fi**sh** on di**sh**

Dear Family Member,

This is a story your child has read at school. Encourage your child to read the story to you, and then talk about it together.

Lunch

Seth had lunch with his mom and dad.
Pat had shrimp and chips.
Ted had shrimp, fish, and chips.
Seth had ham and chips.

Munch, munch.
Crunch, crunch.
Yum, yum.

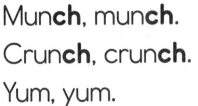

Ask your child to read each of the following words. After he has read each word, ask him to provide a rhyming word.

quit

that

chip

shop

sang

thing

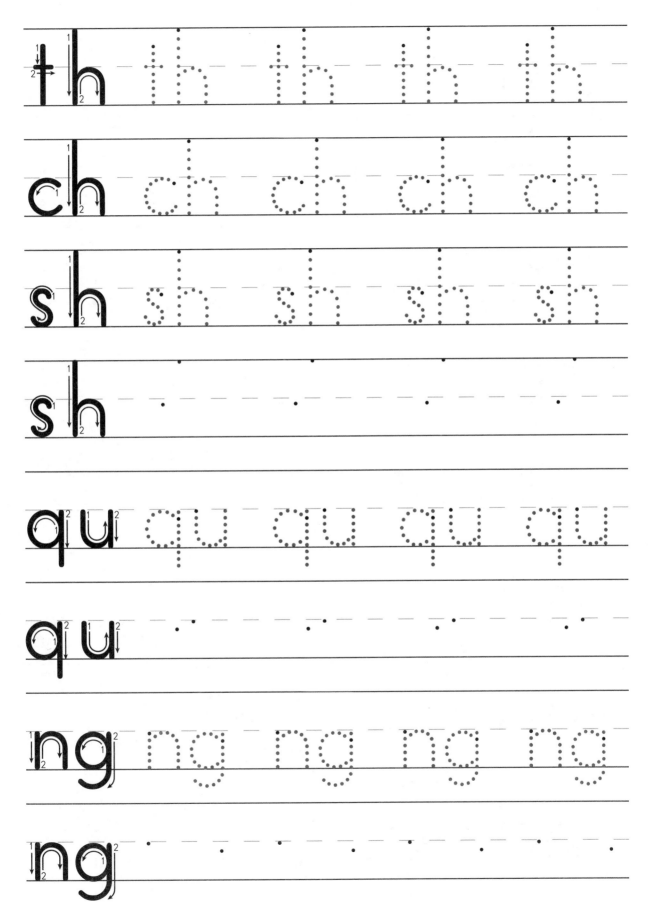

Directions: Have students trace and copy the digraphs as they say the sounds.

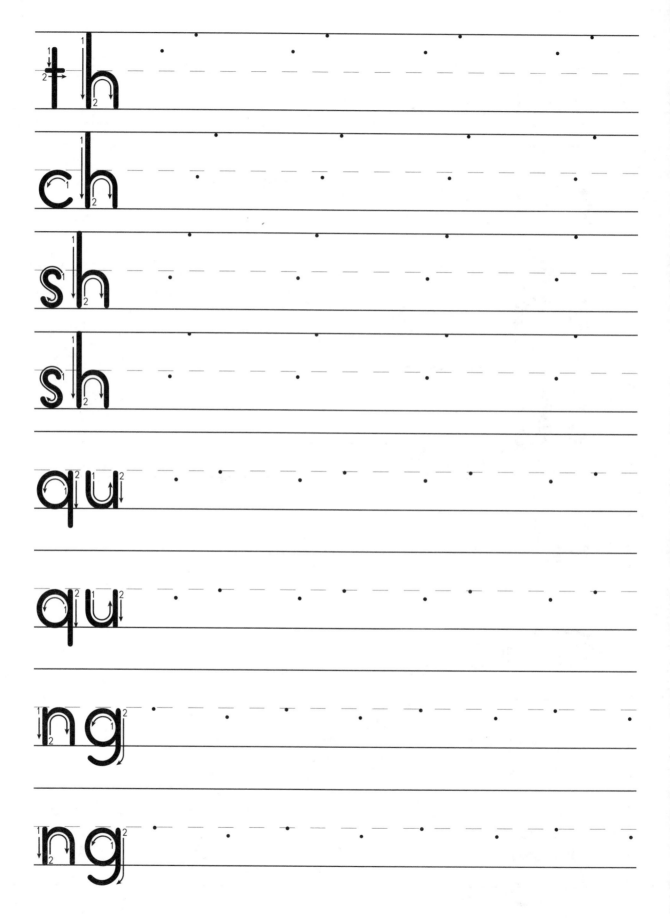

Name _____

Dear Family Member,

Ask your child to cut out the two circles. Pin the smaller circle on top of the larger circle with a brass fastener. Ask your child to spin the smaller circle to make words. Have your child read the words he or she makes. Discuss whether each word is real or silly. Additionally you may ask your child to copy the words on a sheet of paper.

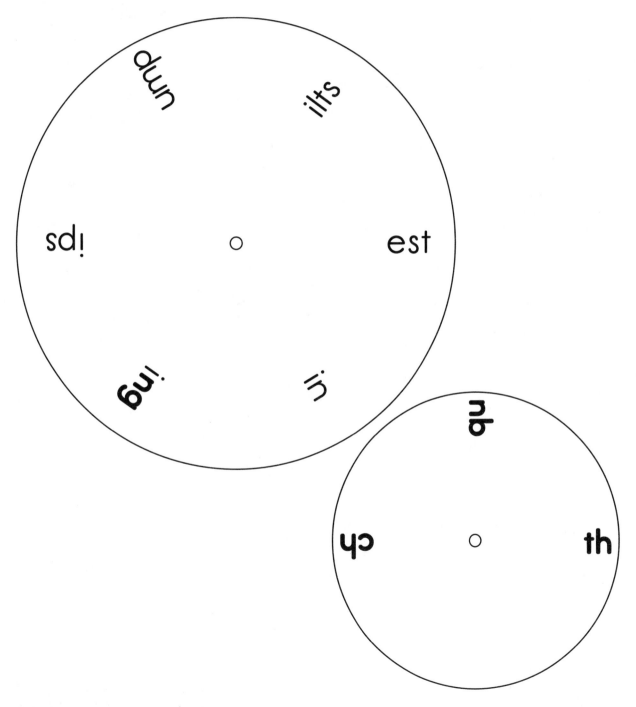

Directions: Have students cut out the word cards and place them on the matching words on Worksheet PP4.

champ	**th**ump	sli**ng**
them	**th**rust	**qu**iz
bru**sh**	**sh**elf	ben**ch**
this	ba**th**s	**sh**eds
quit	**ch**ins	wi**ng**s

Directions: Have students read the word cards from Worksheet PP3 and place them on top of the matching words on this worksheet.

sling	ben**ch**	**ch**amp
quiz	**th**em	**th**ump
sheds	bru**sh**	**th**rust
chins	**th**is	**sh**elf
wi**ng**s	**qu**it	ba**th**s

Directions: For each picture, have students read the phrases and put a check mark in the box next to the matching phrase.

1. ☐ fi**sh** in pan
   ☐ fi**sh** in pond

2. ☐ stro**ng** man
   ☐ **th**in man

3. ☐ bri**ng** lun**ch**
   ☐ bri**ng** gift

4. ☐ man sits at desk
   ☐ man sits on ben**ch**

5. ☐ ants in cup
   ☐ ants in bag

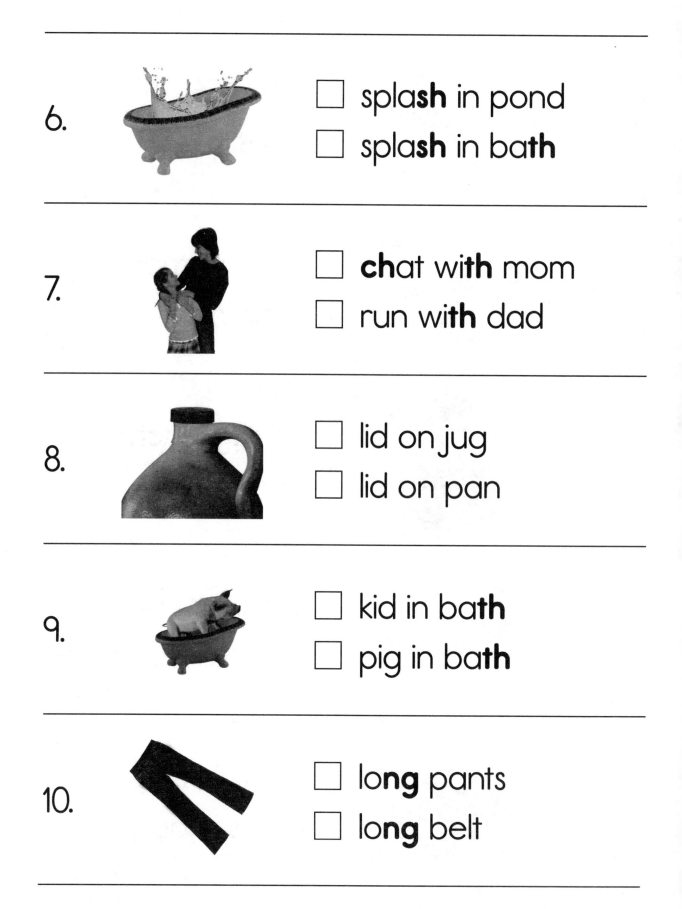

6. ☐ spla**sh** in pond
   ☐ spla**sh** in ba**th**

7. ☐ **ch**at wi**th** mom
   ☐ run wi**th** dad

8. ☐ lid on jug
   ☐ lid on pan

9. ☐ kid in ba**th**
   ☐ pig in ba**th**

10. ☐ lo**ng** pants
    ☐ lo**ng** belt

Dear Family Member,

This is a story your child has read at school. Encourage your child to read the story to you, and then talk about it together.

Seth's Finch

That's Se**th**'s pet fin**ch**,
Chip.
Chip can flap his wi**ng**s.
Chip can mun**ch** on ants and bugs.
Chip can si**ng**.

Chip can land on Se**th**'s hand.
That fin**ch** is fun!

Ask your child to read each of the following words. After he has read each word, ask him to provide a rhyming word.

thin

chest

lunch

wing

dish

math

Lost Finch

Se**th**'s pet fin**ch**, **Ch**ip,
is lost.
Se**th** can't spot him.
Pat can't spot him.
Ted can't spot him.

Chip is not on Se**th**'s bed.
Chip is not on Se**th**'s desk.
Then, at last, Pat spots
Chip.
Chip hid in Pat's hat and
slept.

Dear Family Member,

This is a story your child read at school. Encourage your child to read the story to you, and talk about it together.

Seth's Sled

Seth's sled went fast.
Seth held on.
Seth hit bumps but did
not stop.
Seth hit slush but did
not stop.

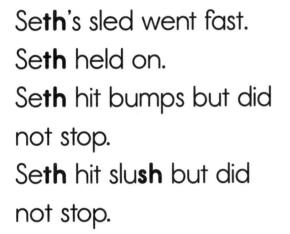

Then Seth's sled hit mud.
Splash!
Seth got mud on his sled.
Seth got mud on his pants.
Seth got mud on his hat.

Dear Family Member,

This is a story your child read at school. Encourage your child to read the story to you, and talk about it together.

Meg's Tots

This is Meg.

Meg is Pat's best pal.

Pat has 1 lad—Se**th**.

Meg has 5 tots—Tom, Tim, Max, Sam, and Wes.

Meg has **qu**ints!

Pat and Ted help Meg.

Pat sets Tim and Tom on Se**th**'s rug.

Ted sets Sam on Se**th**'s **qu**ilt.

Pat sets Max on Se**th**'s bed.

Ted helps Wes stand up on Se**th**'s desk.

Name _____

Dear Family Member,

This is a story your child read at school. Encourage your child to read the story to you, and talk about it together.

Hash and Milk

Pat and Ted had lun**ch** wi**th**

Meg's tots.

Max got ha**sh** on his **ch**in.

Wes got ha**sh** on his bib.

Tim's milk is on Tom.

Then Tom got milk on Tim.

Sam got milk on Pat and Ted.

Dear Family Member,

Ask your child to cut out the letter cards. Show the cards to your child and have him or her say the sounds. (You may also wish to review the letter names.) Additionally, you may arrange the cards to make the words "chin," "chip," "chop," "pinch," "quip," "shin," "ship," "shop," "thin," "thing," "ping," and "pong," and have your child read the words. You may have your child copy the words on a sheet of paper. Additional activity: Say one of the words listed above and ask your child to try and spell the word by selecting and arranging letter cards.

ch	i	n _
qu	sh	p _
ng	th	o

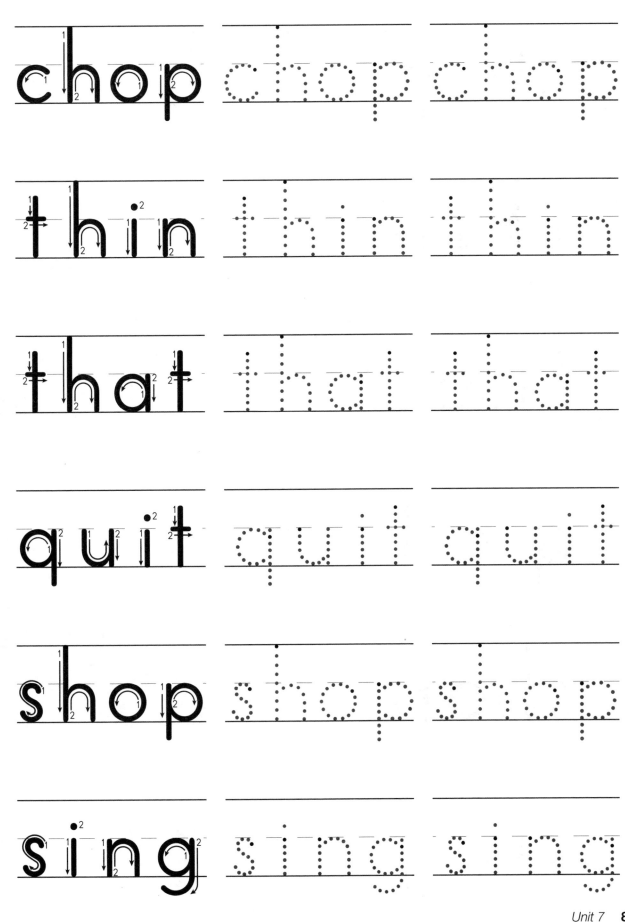

Directions: Have students trace and copy the words as they say the sounds.

1. bran**ch**

2. **sh**ed

3. mo**th**

Directions: Have students write each word under the matching picture.

4. **qu**ilt

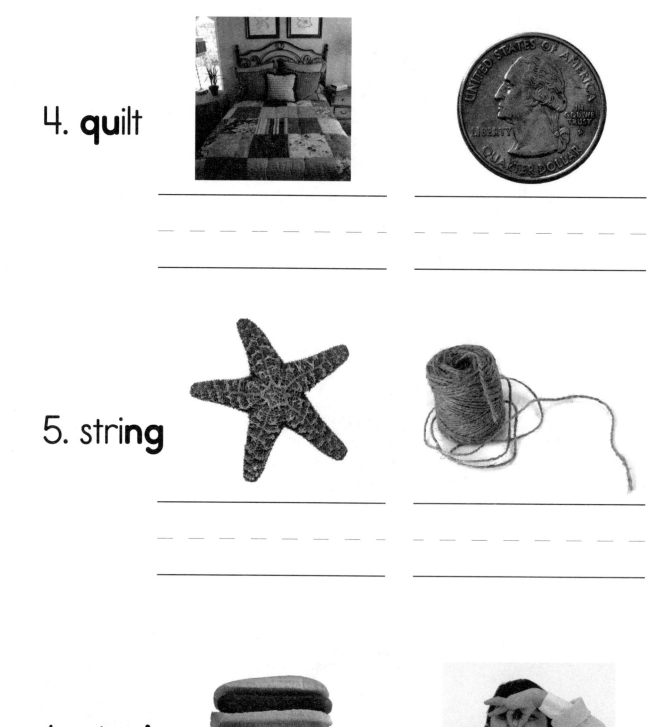

5. stri**ng**

6. pin**ch**

ring	brush	chop
shed	quilt	bath

Directions: Have students write each word under its matching picture.

thumb   sing   chimp

cash   wing   chat

Directions: For each picture, have students circle the spelling of the depicted item and write the name of the item on the line.

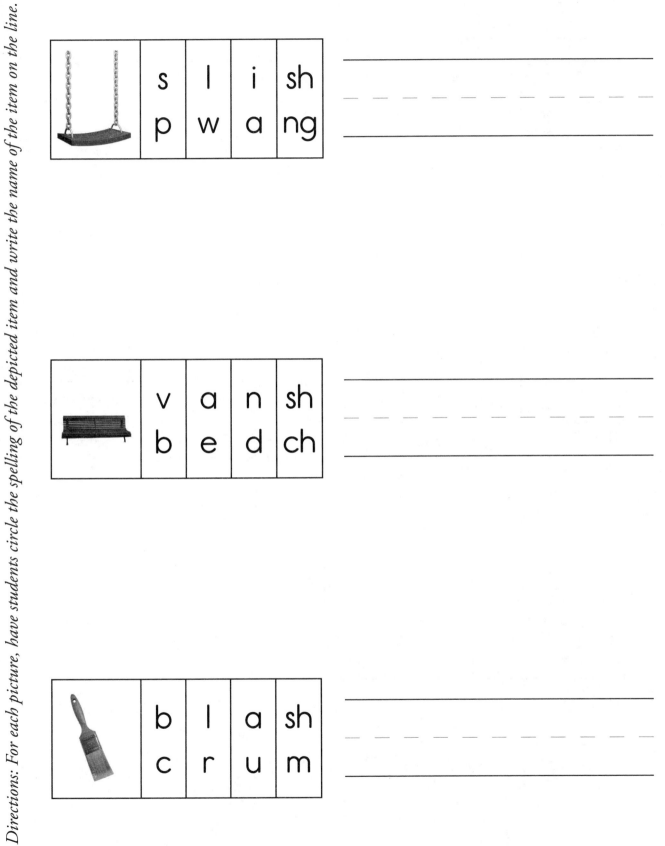

s	l	i	sh
p	w	a	ng

v	a	n	sh
b	e	d	ch

b	l	a	sh
c	r	u	m

qu	i	n	t
p	e	l	m

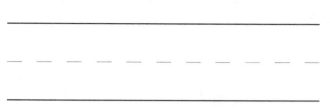

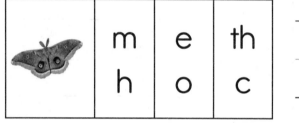

m	e	th
h	o	c

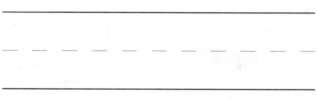

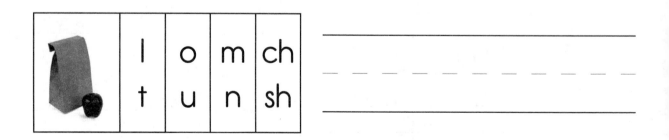

l	o	m	ch
t	u	n	sh

Running Record of "Lost Finch" – As each student reads aloud from the Reader, *Seth*, mark any misread words directly above the word; circle any omitted words.

Lost Finch

Seth's pet finch, Chip, is lost.

Seth can't spot him.

Pat can't spot him.

Ted can't spot him.

Chip is not on Seth's bed.

Chip is not on Seth's desk.

Then, at last, Pat spots Chip.

Chip hid in Pat's hat and slept.

Number of misread words: _____/45

Notes:

Running Record of "Seth's Sled" – As each student reads aloud from the Reader, *Seth*, mark any misread words directly above the word; circle any omitted words.

Seth's Sled

Seth's sled went fast.

Seth held on.

Seth hit bumps but did not stop.

Seth hit slush but did not stop.

Then Seth's sled hit mud.

Splash!

Seth got mud on his sled.

Seth got mud on his pants.

Seth got mud on his hat.

Number of misread words: _____/47

Notes:

Running Record of "Meg's Tots" – As each student reads aloud from the Reader, *Seth*, mark any misread words directly above the word; circle any omitted words.

Meg's Tots

This is Meg.

Meg is Pat's best pal.

Pat has 1 lad – Seth.

Meg has 5 tots – Tom, Tim, Max, Sam, and Wes. Meg has quints!

Pat and Ted help Meg.

Pat sets Tim and Tom on Seth's rug.

Ted sets Sam on Seth's quilt.

Pat sets Max on Seth's bed.

Ted helps Wes stand up on Seth's desk.

Number of misread words: _____/61

Notes:

Running Record of "Hash and Milk" – As each student reads aloud from the Reader, *Seth*, mark any misread words directly above the word; circle any omitted words.

Hash and Milk

Pat and Ted had lunch with Meg's tots.

Max got hash on his chin.

Wes got hash on his bib.

Tim's milk is on Tom.

Then Tom got milk on Tim.

Sam got milk on Pat and Ted.

Number of misread words: _____/41

Notes:

CORE KNOWLEDGE LANGUAGE ARTS

SERIES EDITOR-IN-CHIEF
E. D. Hirsch, Jr.

PRESIDENT
Linda Bevilacqua

EDITORIAL STAFF
Carolyn Gosse, Senior Editor - Preschool
Khara Turnbull, Materials Development Manager
Michelle L. Warner, Senior Editor - Listening & Learning

Mick Anderson
Robin Blackshire
Maggie Buchanan
Paula Coyner
Sue Fulton
Sara Hunt
Erin Kist
Robin Luecke
Rosie McCormick
Cynthia Peng
Liz Pettit
Ellen Sadler
Deborah Samley
Diane Auger Smith
Sarah Zelinke

DESIGN AND GRAPHICS STAFF
Scott Ritchie, Creative Director

Kim Berrall
Michael Donegan
Liza Greene
Matt Leech
Bridget Moriarty
Lauren Pack

CONSULTING PROJECT MANAGEMENT SERVICES
ScribeConcepts.com

ADDITIONAL CONSULTING SERVICES
Ang Blanchette
Dorrit Green
Carolyn Pinkerton

ACKNOWLEDGMENTS

These materials are the result of the work, advice, and encouragement of numerous individuals over many years. Some of those singled out here already know the depth of our gratitude; others may be surprised to find themselves thanked publicly for help they gave quietly and generously for the sake of the enterprise alone. To helpers named and unnamed we are deeply grateful.

CONTRIBUTORS TO EARLIER VERSIONS OF THESE MATERIALS

Susan B. Albaugh, Kazuko Ashizawa, Nancy Braier, Kathryn M. Cummings, Michelle De Groot, Diana Espinal, Mary E. Forbes, Michael L. Ford, Ted Hirsch, Danielle Knecht, James K. Lee, Diane Henry Leipzig, Martha G. Mack, Liana Mahoney, Isabel McLean, Steve Morrison, Juliane K. Munson, Elizabeth B. Rasmussen, Laura Tortorelli, Rachael L. Shaw, Sivan B. Sherman, Miriam E. Vidaver, Catherine S. Whittington, Jeannette A. Williams

We would like to extend special recognition to Program Directors Matthew Davis and Souzanne Wright who were instrumental to the early development of this program.

SCHOOLS

We are truly grateful to the teachers, students, and administrators of the following schools for their willingness to field test these materials and for their invaluable advice: Capitol View Elementary, Challenge Foundation Academy (IN), Community Academy Public Charter School, Lake Lure Classical Academy, Lepanto Elementary School, New Holland Core Knowledge Academy, Paramount School of Excellence, Pioneer Challenge Foundation Academy, New York City PS 26R (The Carteret School), PS 30X (Wilton School), PS 50X (Clara Barton School), PS 96Q, PS 102X (Joseph O. Loretan), PS 104Q (The Bays Water), PS 214K (Michael Friedsam), PS 223Q (Lyndon B. Johnson School), PS 308K (Clara Cardwell), PS 333Q (Goldie Maple Academy), Sequoyah Elementary School, South Shore Charter Public School, Spartanburg Charter School, Steed Elementary School, Thomas Jefferson Classical Academy, Three Oaks Elementary, West Manor Elementary.

And a special thanks to the CKLA Pilot Coordinators Anita Henderson, Yasmin Lugo-Hernandez, and Susan Smith, whose suggestions and day-to-day support to teachers using these materials in their classrooms was critical.

CREDITS

ILLUSTRATORS AND IMAGE SOURCES